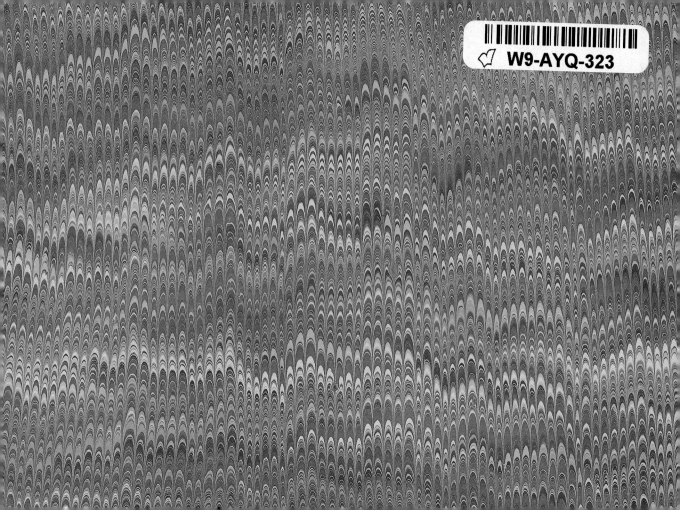

SPIRIT OF PLACE
❖ ROME ❖

First among cities, the home of gods, is Golden Rome.

AUSONIUS, *ORDO URBIUM NOBILIUM*, 4TH CENTURY AD

Arcade Publishing · New York

Little, Brown and Company

The First Sight of Rome

I could have spent the whole day by the rivulet, lost in dreams and meditations; but recollecting my vow, I ran back to the carriage and drove on. The road not having been mended, I believe, since the days of the Caesars, would not allow our motions to be very precipitate, 'When you gain the summit of yonder hill, you will discover Rome,' said one of the postilions: up we dragged; no city appeared. 'From the next,' cried out a second; and so on from height to height did they amuse my expectations. I thought Rome fled before us, such was my impatience, till at last we perceived a cluster of hills with green pastures on their summits, inclosed by thickets and shaded by flourishing ilex. Here and there a white house, built in the antique style, with open porticos, that received a faint gleam of the evening sun, just emerged from the clouds and tinting the meads below. Now domes and towers began to discover themselves in the valley, and St Peter's to rise above the magnificent roofs of the Vatican. Every step we advanced the scene extended, till, winding suddenly round the hill, all Rome opened to our view.

WILLIAM BECKFORD, *ITALY*, 1834

ARRIVING IN ROME

A bridge was immediately in front. It was adorned with statues in soft stone, half-eaten away, but still gesticulating in corruption, after the manner of the seventeenth century. Beneath the bridge there tumbled and swelled and ran fast a great confusion of yellow water: it was the Tiber. Far on the right were white barracks of huge and of hideous appearance; over these the dome of St Peter's rose and looked like something newly built. It was of a delicate blue, but made a metallic contrast against the sky. . . I went on for several hundred yards, having the old wall of Rome before me all the time, till I came right under it at last; and with the hesitation that befits all great actions I entered, putting the right foot first lest I should bring further misfortune upon that capital of all our fortunes.

And so the journey ended.

HILAIRE BELLOC, *THE PATH TO ROME*, 1902

A FIRST DAY IN ROME

A first day in Rome is always an event. Soaking up the wonderful golden umber, the brown-orange of its unique colour touched up by silver-grey of church and palace stone. This is a city which writes SPQR on its draincovers. This is where in the early 1900s a bored Society took its rollerskates out to dinner, and skated round the gloomy stone corridors of their renaissance and baroque palaces – envy of all tourist feet. In Rome, among more sublime happenings of which we have all read so much, we may find the first papal railway train, built only to travel the short stretch to nearby Gandolfo, and made up of three gilded carriages with wooden buffers, one carriage an open canopy for blessings, one a little chapel . . . And it is a pleasure in Rome to go to the opera, possibly mediocre but gay with many different kinds of police in gala uniforms, and see *Tosca* with its settings of San Andrea and the Farnese Palace and the Castello San Angelo, all of which we have tramped round during the day.

WILLIAM SANSOM, *GRAND TOUR TODAY*, 1968

From Capitol to Coliseo

From the Capitol to the Coliseo, including the Forum Romanum and Boarium, there is nothing entire but one or two churches, built with the fragments of ancient edifices. You descend from the Capitol between the remaining pillars of two temples, the pedestals and part of the shafts sunk in the rubbish: then passing through the triumphal arch of Septimius Severus, you proceed along the foot of Mons Palatinus, which stands on your right hand, quite covered with the ruins of the ancient palace belonging to the Roman emperors, and at the foot of it, there are some beautiful detached pillars still standing . . . Farther on, is the Arch of Constantine on the right, a most noble piece of architecture, almost entire; with the remains of the *Meta Sudans* before it; and fronting you, the noble ruins of that vast amphitheatre, called the Colossaeum, now Coliseo, which has been dismantled and dilapidated by the Gothic popes and princes of modern Rome, to build and adorn their paultry palaces.

TOBIAS SMOLLETT, *TRAVELS THROUGH FRANCE AND ITALY*, 1766

To delight in the aspects of *sentient* ruin might appear a heartless pastime, and the pleasure, I confess, shows the note of perversity. The sombre and the hard are as common an influence from southern things as the soft and the bright, I think; sadness rarely fails to assault a northern observer when he misses what he takes for comfort. Beauty is no compensation for the loss, only making it more poignant. Enough beauty of climate hangs over these Roman cottages and farm-houses – beauty of light, of atmosphere and of vegetation; but their charm for the maker-out of the stories in things is the way the golden air shows off their desolation. Man lives more with Nature in Italy than in New or than in Old England; she does more work for him and gives him more holidays than in our short-summered climes, and his home is therefore much more bare of devices for helping him to do without her, forget her and forgive her.

HENRY JAMES, *ITALIAN HOURS*, 1909

THE COLISEUM

I see a great circle of arches built upon arches, and shattered stones lie around, that once made a part of the solid wall. In the crevices, and on the vaulted roofs, grow a multitude of shrubs, the wild olive and the myrtle – and intricate brambles, and entangled weeds and plants I never saw before. The stones are immensely massive, and they jut out one from the other. There are terrible rifts in the wall, and broad windows through which you see the blue heaven. There seems to be more than a thousand arches, some ruined, some entire, and they are all immensely high and wide. Some are shattered, and stand forth in great heaps, and the underwood is tufted on their crumbling summits. Around us lie enormous columns, shattered and shapeless – and fragments of capitals and cornice, fretted with delicate sculptures.

PERCY BYSSHE SHELLEY, *ESSAYS*

THE ARCH OF CONSTANTINE

After having taken a few steps toward the Colosseum, we saw Constantine's arch to our right. The mass of this monument is imposing and fine; it has three arcades, like that of the Carrousel, with which we find it to have many points of resemblance; it is adorned on each façade by four fluted columns of antique yellow and of Corinthian order which bear statues.

It is evident that Constantine had the weakness to have this triumphal arch, which had been erected to Trajan, arranged in his own honour. Thus is explained the beauty of the general plan, which clashes with the poor execution of several details. The Roman character, broken and debased by the reign of a succession of monsters, betrayed its degradation by the decadence of the arts. This monument was erected about the year 326; the inscription announces that it was meant to celebrate the victory won by Constantine over Maxentius . . . It is singular that so useless a thing should give such great pleasure; the style of the triumphal arch is an architectural conquest.

STENDHAL, *A ROMAN JOURNAL*, 1829

ANCIENT AND MODERN ROME

But whether, in this ride, you pass by obelisks, or columns: ancient temples, theatres, houses, porticos, or forums: it is strange to see, how every fragment, whenever it is possible, has been blended into some modern structure, and made to serve some modern purpose – a wall, a dwelling-place, a granary, a stable – some use for which it never was designed, and associated with which it cannot otherwise than lamely assort. It is stranger still, to see how many ruins of the old mythology: how many fragments of obsolete legend and observance: have been incorporated into the worship of Christian altars here; and how, in numberless respects, the false faith and the true are fused into a monstrous union.

CHARLES DICKENS, *PICTURES FROM ITALY*, 1846

THE COLOURS OF ROME

The great beauty of these landscapes is that objects which are vividly coloured, even if they are only a little distance away, are softened by the atmosphere, and that the contrasts of cold and warm tones, as they are called, are so pronounced. The clear blue shadows stand out delightfully against anything green, yellow, red or brown, and merge into the bluish haze of the distance. There is a brilliance and at the same time a subtly graded harmony which one can hardly conceive up in the north, where everything is either harsh or indistinct, either too bright or too drab. At least, I rarely remember having seen an effect which could have given me an inkling of what I see here every day.

J. W. GOETHE, *ITALIAN JOURNEY*, 1786–88

Henrik I. 1897-1911

THE TREVI FOUNTAIN

In the side streets at the lower end of the Via del Tritone, you hear a steady sound of falling water. It is an arresting sound in a city, for it is not the polite whisper of a fountain, but the untamed roar of glen or mountain water. It is almost as though the Pass of Killiecrankie were visiting Rome. If you follow this sound through the narrow streets, it will lead you to the most spectacular fountain in Rome, and now its most popular sight, the Fontana di Trevi . . .

This masque of water, though it is not my favourite Roman fountain, is one which constantly delights and surprises by its audacious fantasy. The idea of transposing a rocky landscape gushing with waterfalls, with Neptune and his steeds in violent action, upon the sedate and formal façade of a Renaissance palace is itself such a startling improbability that one stands amazed. It seems to me so characteristic of Rome that this romantic vision should be tucked away behind narrow streets, and in a piazza only just large enough to contain it. Where but in Rome would anyone have dreamed of erecting such a monument in such a place?

H. V. MORTON, *A TRAVELLER IN ROME*, 1957

St Peter's

But lo! the dome – the vast and wondrous dome,
To which Diana's marvel was a cell –
Christ's mighty shrine above his martyr's tomb!
I have beheld the Ephesian's miracle –
Its columns strew the wilderness, and dwell
The hyaenia and the jackal in their shade;
I have beheld Sophia's bright roofs swell
Their glittering mass i' the sun, and have survey'd
Its sanctuary the while the usurping Moslem pray'd;

But thou, of temples old, or altars new,
Standest alone – with nothing like to thee –
Worthiest of God, the holy and the true,
Since Zion's desolation, when that He
Forsook His former city, what could be,
Of earthly structures, in His honour piled,
Of a sublimer aspect? Majesty,
Power, Glory, Strength, and Beauty, all are aisled
In this eternal ark of worship undefiled.

LORD BYRON, *CHILDE HAROLD'S PILGRIMAGE*, 1816

WITHIN ST PETER'S

St Peter's looks fairly large, but it is very much larger than it looks ... Something in the curious cavernous lines of the place, with its wide and curved and almost wavering pillars, makes us imagine something lowering over our heads or enclosing us in dizzy and magic circles, which is not the same as the mere sensation of unlimited space. There is a sort of optical illusion, which is here corrected by what I may call an auricular confession. Suddenly, I realized that my ears contradicted my eyes. For there came as if carried on the wind something that was almost a whisper; and yet I knew by the thrill of it that it was a shout. It was the people at the other end of the church cheering the Pope; but it was like the sound of people cheering whole streets away. . . It was as if a man called across the room and his voice seemed to come faint and far across the valley. And with the sound of that the whole building seemed to

swell and expand and open upwards into eternity, until we realized that these painted and gilded caverns were vast like the hollows of the sky. The noise grew louder and louder along a remote and winding road; and at last, while it was yet distant, rose into one deafening roar of 'Viva Il Papa'.

G. K. CHESTERTON, *THE RESURRECTION OF ROME*, 1930

The Vatican has several parts that are architecturally very fine, ten thousand rooms and no façade. One must look under the colonnade of St Peter's for the door that leads to it. At the end of the round part of the colonnade to the right the traveller notices certain grotesque figures clad in strips of yellow, red and blue material; these are good Swiss armed with pikes and dressed in uniforms such as were worn in the fifteenth century. The Swiss at that time composed one-half of all the infantry of Europe, and the brave half; from this came the usage of having a Swiss guard.

A dark and very fine stairway, which is at the end of the porch of St Peter's, leads to the entrance to the Vatican. During Holy Week it is illuminated with an admirable magnificence; the rest of the year it is solitary. You ring a bell before a door of worm-eaten wood, and after ten minutes an old woman comes and opens it; you find yourself in an immense antichamber; it is the *Sala reale*, which serves as a vestibule to the Sistine and Pauline chapels.

STENDHAL, *A ROMAN JOURNAL*, 1829

THE VILLA MEDICI

With S. to the Villa Medici – perhaps on the whole the most enchanting place in Rome. The part of the garden called the Boschetto has an incredible, impossible charm; an upper terrace, behind locked gates, covered with a little dusky forest of evergreen oaks. Such a dim light as of a fabled, haunted place, such a soft suffusion of tender grey-green tones, such a company of gnarled and twisted little miniature trunks – dwarfs playing with each other at being giants – and such a shower of golden sparkles drifting in from the vivid west! At the end of the wood is a steep, circular mound, up which the short trees scramble amain, with a long mossy staircase climbing up to a belvedere. This staircase, rising suddenly out of the leafy dusk to you don't see where, is delightfully fantastic. . . The Villa Medici has distilled an essence of its own – walled it in and made it delightfully private. The great façade on the gardens is like an enormous rococo clock-face all incrusted with images and arabesques and tablets. What mornings and afternoons one might spend there, brush in hand, unpreoccupied, untormented, pensioned, satisfied. . .

HENRY JAMES, *ITALIAN HOURS*, 1909

THE SPANISH STEPS

Among what may be called the Cubs or minor Lions of Rome, there was one that amused me mightily. It is always to be found there; and its den is on the great flight of steps that lead from the Piazza di Spagna, to the church of Trinita del Monte. In plainer words, these steps are the great place of resort for the artists' 'Models', and there they are constantly waiting to be hired. The first time I went up there, I could not conceive why the faces seemed familiar to me; why they appeared to have beset me, for years, in every possible variety of action and costume; and how it came to pass that they started up before me, in Rome, in the broad day, like so many saddled and bridled nightmares. I soon found that we had made acquaintance, and improved it, for several years, on the walls of various Exhibition Galleries. There is one old gentleman, with long, white hair and an immense beard, who, to my knowledge, has gone half through the catalogue of the Royal Academy.

CHARLES DICKENS, *PICTURES FROM ITALY*, 1846

Nothing can be more agreeable to the eyes of a stranger, especially in the heats of summer, than the great number of public fountains that appear in every part of Rome, embellished with all the ornaments of sculpture, and pouring forth prodigious quantities of cool, delicious water, brought in aqueducts from different lakes, rivers, and sources, at a considerable distance from the city. These works are the remains of the munificence and industry of the ancient Romans, who were extremely delicate in the art of water: but, however, great applause is also due to those benificent popes who have been at the expense of restoring and repairing those noble channels of health, pleasure, and convenience. This great plenty of water, nevertheless, has not induced the Romans to be cleanly. Their streets, and even their palaces, are disgraced with filth. The noble Piazza Navona is adorned with three or four fountains, one of which is perhaps the most magnificent in Europe, and all of them discharge vast streams of water: but, notwithstanding this provision, the piazza is almost as dirty as West Smithfield.

TOBIAS SMOLLETT, *TRAVELS THROUGH FRANCE AND ITALY*, 1766

THE VILLA BORGHESE

The smile of Rome, as I have called it, and its insidious message to those who incline to ramble irresponsibly and take things as they come, is ushered in with the first breath of spring, and then it grows and grows with the advancing season till it wraps the whole place in its tenfold charm. As the process develops you can do few better things than go often to Villa Borghese and sit on the grass – on a stout bit of drapery – and watch its exquisite stages. It has a frankness and a sweetness beyond any relenting of *our* clumsy climates even when ours leave off their damnable faces and begin. Nature departs from every reserve with a confidence that leaves one at a loss where, as it were, to look – leaves one, as I say, nothing to do but to lay one's head among the anemones at the base of a high-stemmed pine and gaze up crestward and skyward along its slanting silvery column. You may watch the whole business from a dozen of these choice standpoints and have a different villa for it every day in the week . . . But I prefer none of them to the Borghese, which is free to all the world at all times and yet never crowded.

HENRY JAMES, *ITALIAN HOURS*, 1909

CASTEL ST ANGELO

The emperor Hadrian had a real passion for architecture; this is well shown by the vestiges of the famous Villa Adriana, on the road to Tivoli. It was recognized in his time that there was no more room in Augustus's mausoleum for the emperor's ashes. Hadrian seized this occasion to build himself a tomb. He chose the part of the immense Domitia gardens closest to the Tiber, and this edifice was the wonder of his century.

The immense round tower that we see today was, as it were, the nucleus of the building. It was surrounded by a corridor and by another wall that served as a façade. All this has disappeared. Above this round part, according to usage, rose immense steps, and the edifice was crowned by a magnificent temple, also round in form. Twenty-four columns of violet marble formed a portico around this temple; finally, at the highest point of the cupola, was placed the colossal pine cone that has given its name to one of the gardens in the Vatican, and which we have seen there. It was in this bronze tomb that the ashes of one of the most brilliant men ever to occupy a throne were deposited.

STENDHAL, *A ROMAN JOURNAL*, 1829

THE CAMPIDOGLIO

The Capitol hill is the first of the seven hills of Ancient Rome. With the other hills it was deserted in the Middle Ages, but the Capitol was rediscovered in Renaissance times and contains, in addition to the modern monument, some interesting associations with history and art. Behind the monument, approached by a separate stairway, is the church of Santa Maria in Aracoeli, with a beautiful ceiling and some fine Renaissance sculptures. By yet another stairway one may climb to the Campidoglio Square, which may be considered the most beautiful piece of urban planning ever achieved. Across an open space paved in a geometrical design of marble is the Senatorial Palace, the city hall of Rome; its fine sixteenth-century façade dominated by an elegant clock tower and its main entrance approached by two symmetrical stairways framing one of the most attractive of Roman fountains. But it is perhaps the arrangement of the lateral buildings, disposed so as to converge gently towards the entrance stairway, which constitutes the supreme distinction of the planning.

JASPER MORE, *THE LAND OF ITALY*, 1949

SOUVENIRS OF ROME

Sunset found me near the Vatican, in the ward called here the Leonine city, streets inhabited by vendors of prints, rosaries, and souvenirs of Rome: they are all a very Catholic people, who never go to mass, and who swear by the Madonna, and always vote for the Catholic candidate, because one must show gratitude, and, as they say with a wink of the eye, they eat from the *sacra bottega*, the name they give to the palace of the Pope.

V. B. IABAÑEZ, *IN THE LAND OF ART*, 1923

Nobody who has not taken one can imagine the beauty of a walk through Rome by full moon. All details are swallowed up by the huge masses of light and shadow, and only the biggest and most general outlines are visible. We have just enjoyed three clear and glorious nights. The Colosseum looked especially beautiful. It is closed at night. A hermit lives in a small chapel and some beggars have made themselves at home in the crumbling vaults. These had built a fire on the level ground and a gentle breeze had driven the smoke into the arena, so that the lower parts of the ruins were veiled and only the huge masses above loomed out of the darkness. We stood at the railing and watched, while over our heads the moon stood high and serene. By degrees the smoke escaped through holes and crannies and in the moonlight it looked like fog. It was a marvellous sight. This is the kind of illumination by which to see the Pantheon, the Capitol, the square in front of St Peter's, and many other large squares and streets.

Like the human spirit, the sun and the moon have a quite different task to perform here than they have in other places, for here their glance is returned by gigantic, solid masses.

J. W. GOETHE, *ITALIAN JOURNEY*, 1786–1788

'ISLANDS OF SPACE'

Rome is a city of shadows . . . But the greatest shadow of all is its Past. You are not a day in Rome until you feel its mesmerism. At every turn you are spirited away to the far-off days when the modern world was in the making. The shroud of an awesome silence enwraps those buried ruins.

One moment you are in the midst of life, noise, the rush of the Twentieth Century; the next you have rounded a corner, and there the skeleton of decayed glory confronts you in the colonnaded ribs of vanished temples, in the broken joints of stately palaces. The hum of To-day dies away, and on your ear falls in ghostly whispers the accents of a mighty Yesterday. . .

Old Rome is a city of corners. The short, narrow streets break off at sharp angles, often leaving odd little squares, islands of space in an over-shadowing mass of masonry. These breathing spots teem with life and interest. In these picturesque eddies old customs still lurk. They are outside the great stream of the modern thoroughfare, and have not been swept into the current of progress. You step into the past when you penetrate the shadows of those narrow lanes. Yesterday still lingers there.

A. G. MacKinnon, *Things Seen in Rome*, 1934

ON THE APPIAN WAY

Here was Rome indeed at last; and such a Rome as no one can imagine in its full and awful grandeur! We wandered out upon the Appian Way, and then went on, through miles of ruined tombs and broken walls, with here and there a desolate and uninhabited house: past the Circus of Romulus, where the course of the chariots, the stations of the judges, competitors, and spectators, are yet as plainly to be seen as in old time: past the tomb of Cecilia Metella: past all inclosure, hedge, or stake, wall or fence: away upon the open Campagna, where on that side of Rome, nothing is to be beheld but Ruin. Except where the distant Apennines bound the view upon the left, the whole wide prospect is one field of ruin. Broken aqueducts, left in the most picturesque and beautiful clusters of arches; broken temples; broken tombs. A desert of decay, sombre and desolate beyond all expression; and with a history in every stone that strews the ground.

CHARLES DICKENS, *PICTURES FROM ITALY*, 1846

A RENAISSANCE PLEASURE-HOUSE

January 30th. – A drive the other day with a friend to Villa Madama, on the side of Monte Mario . . . What a grim commentary on history such a scene – what an irony of the past! The 'feature' is the contents of the loggia: a vaulted roof and walls decorated by Giulio Romano; exquisite stucco-work and still brilliant frescoes; arabesques and figurini, nymphs and fauns, animals and flowers – gracefully lavish designs of every sort. Much of the colour – especially the blues – still almost vivid, and all the work wonderfully ingenious, elegant and charming. Apartments so decorated can have been meant only for the recreation of people greater than any we know, people for whom life was impudent ease and success. Margaret Farnese was the lady of the house, but where she trailed her cloth of gold the chickens now scamper between your legs over rotten straw.

HENRY JAMES, *ITALIAN HOURS*, 1909

TIVOLI

Tivoli, the Roman Tibur so much praised by Horace, is situated on the left bank of the River Aniene at the point where the river hurls itself down the steep slopes of the Apennine foothills to the level of the Roman plain. Diversions of water for industrial purposes have impaired the beauty of its famous waterfalls, but it is still worthwhile to make the tour of the Panoramic Road. The town itself is a warren of narrow and not very attractive streets but contains, on the edge of the Aniene gorge, well-preserved ruins of two Roman temples approachable through the garden of an hotel. On the outside of the town is the Villa d'Este, perhaps the best known of all the sumptuous Renaissance villas so characteristic of the environs of Rome. While the villa itself is scarcely comparable with such masterpieces as Caprarola, the garden, thanks to its compact design and good preservation, is perhaps the most impressive of all these beautiful creations. Amidst beautifully disposed pines and cypresses one descends by paths and terraces to the various garden levels, each of which is enlivened by an exquisitely conceived arrangement of rivulets or fountains.

JASPER MORE, *THE LAND OF ITALY*, 1949

FAREWELL TO ROME

Day after day and night after night we have wandered among the crumbling wonders of Rome; day after day and night after night we have fed upon the dust and decay of five-and-twenty centuries – have brooded over them by day and dreamt of them by night till sometimes we seemed mouldering away ourselves, and growing defaced and cornerless, and liable at any moment to fall a prey to some antiquary and be patched in the legs, and 'restored' with an unseemly nose, and labelled wrong and dated wrong, and set up in the Vatican for poets to drivel about and vandals to scribble their names on for ever and for ever more.

But the surest way to stop writing about Rome is to stop. I wished to write a real 'guide-book' chapter on this fascinating city, but I could not do it, because I have felt all the time like a boy in a candy-shop – there was everything to choose from, and yet no choice. I have drifted along hopelessly without knowing where to commence. I will not commence at all.

MARK TWAIN, *THE INNOCENTS ABROAD*, 1869

ACKNOWLEDGEMENTS

PICTURE CREDITS

Front cover/5: *A View of Rome with the Bridge and Castel St Angelo*, Gaspare Vanvitelli (Roy Miles Fine Paintings/Bridgeman Art Library – hereafter BAL)
Back cover: *The Forum*, Gustav Palm (Bonhams/BAL)
Frontispiece: *Sunset from Trinità dei Monti*, Henri Joseph Harpignies (Musée des Beaux-Arts, Rouen/Lauros-Giraudon)
3: *Rome, On the Grand Tour*, W. J. Jones (David Ker Fine Art/BAL)
7: *View of Rome*, John Heseltine
9: *The Forum*, David Roberts (Guildhall Art Gallery/BAL)
10: *At the Museo dei Conservatori*, Giancarlo Gasponi
11: *House of the Vestal Virgins*, Josef Theodor Hansen (Christie's Colour Library)
13: *The Forum*, Augustus Hare (Chris Beetles Ltd)
15: *The Colosseum and Arch of Constantine*, John Heseltine
16: *Fragments of the Statue of Constantine, Museo dei Conservatori*, Giancarlo Gasponi
17: *Trinità dei Monti and the Villa Medici*, M. Granet (Louvre/Scala)
19: *The Palatine Hill*, Henrik Jesperson (Christie's Colour Library)
21: *Trevi Fountain*, Fernando Bueno (Image Bank)
23: *Exterior of St Peter's from the Piazza*, Louis Haghe (Victoria & Albert Museum/BAL)
24: *Statue of Arnolfo di Cambio, St Peter's*, Giancarlo Gasponi
25: *Interior of St Peter's During A Ceremony*, Anon. (Citta del Vaticanno, Ufficio Direzione/Scala)
26: *Nuns at the Vatican*, Brett Froomer (Image Bank)
27: *Vatican, Easter Day*, G. Colliva (Image Bank)
29: *Villa Medici*, Gaspare Vanvitelli (Galleria Palatina, Florence/Scala)
31: *Piazza di Spagna*, William Walcot (Chris Beetles Ltd/BAL)
33: *Via Condotti*, Brett Froomer (Image Bank)
34: *Piazza Navona*, John Heseltine

35: *Piazza Navona*, Giovanni Paolo Pannini (Musée des Beaux-Arts, Nantes/BAL/Giraudon)
37: *View of Villa Borghese*, Johann Wilhelm Baur (Galleria Borghese/Scala)
39: *Castel St Angelo*, Eilif Petersen (Christie's Colour Library)
41: *The Campidoglio*, John Newberry (Chris Beetles Ltd)
43: *S. Carlo ai Catinari*, Luigi Serra (Galleria Arte Moderne, Galleria d'Arte Moderna, Florence/Scala)
44: *Above the Spanish Steps*, John Heseltine
45: *Colosseum by Moonlight*, Giancarlo Gasponi
47: *Piazza Barberini*, Gustav Palm (Fine Art Photographs)
49: *Via Appia Antica*, Salomon Corrodi (Christie's Colour Library)
51: *Villa Madama*, Hubert Robert (Hermitage/Scala)
53: *Maecena's Villa near Tivoli*, Thomas Dessoulavy (Christie's Colour Library)
55: *View of Rome from the Villa Medici*, Auguste Numano (Christie's Colour Library)

TEXT CREDITS

Text extracts from the following sources are reproduced with the kind permission of the publishers and copyright holders stated. Should any copyright holder have been inadvertently omitted they should apply to the publishers who will be pleased to credit them in full in any subsequent editions.

4: Hillaire Belloc, *The Path to Rome* (Thomas Nelson, 1902); 6: William Sansom, *Grand Tour Today* (Hogarth Press, 1968); 20: H. V. Morton, *A Traveller in Rome* (Methuen, 1957); 32: Charles FitzRoy, *Italy, A Grand Tour for Modern Travellers* (Macmillan, 1991); 40, 52: Jasper More, *The Land of Italy* (Batsford, 1949); 46: A. G. MacKinnon, *Things Seen in Rome* (Seeley, Service, 1934).

First U.S. Edition

ISBN 1-55970-162-5

Library of Congress Catalog Card Number 91-55226
Library of Congress Cataloging-in-Publication information
is available.

Published in the United States by Arcade Publishing, Inc.,
New York, a Little, Brown company

10   9   8   7   6   5   4   3   2   1

Conceived, edited and designed by Russell Ash & Bernard Higton
Text research by Steve Dobell
Picture research by Mary-Jane Gibson

Printed in Spain

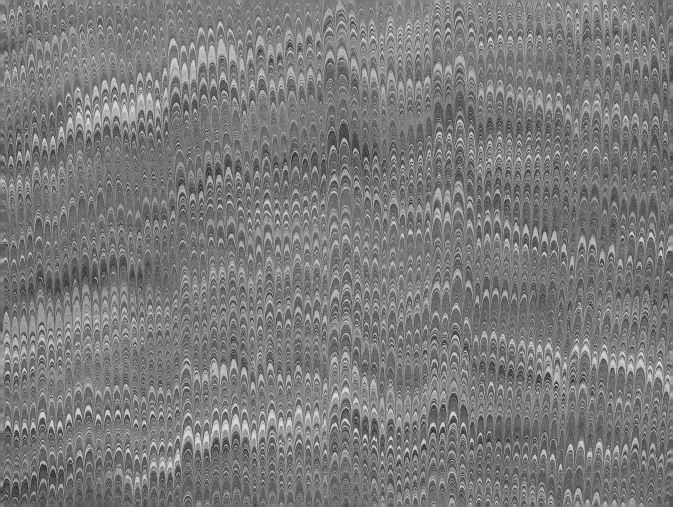